LATE AT NIGHT IN THE ROWBOAT

# LATE AT NIGHT
# IN THE ROWBOAT

poems

## Donald Junkins

LOST HORSE PRESS
Sandpoint · Idaho

ACKNOWLEDGMENT

The "Hawkesbury River" sequence in Part I won the 2004 *New Letters* Poetry Prize; sixteen of the 2001 Swan's Island sonnet sequence appeared as a group titled "Red Point Journal" in the *North Dakota Quarterly*; and other poems appeared in *New Letters, Willow Springs, The Northstone Review,* and *The Hemingway Newsletter.*

*First Edition*

Cover Art: Guy Wiggins
Author Photo: University of Massachusetts staff photo
Book Design: Christine Holbert

*This and other fine Lost Horse Press titles may be viewed on our web site at*
www.losthorsepress.org

LIBRARY OF CONGRESS CATALOGING-IN-PUBLICATION DATA

Junkins, Donald, 1931-
Late at night in the rowboat : poems / Donald Junkins.—1st ed.
p. cm.
ISBN 0-9717265-8-2 (alk. paper)
I. Title.
PS3560.U6L38 2005
811'.54—dc22

2004026361

FOR KAIMEI AND YUNWEI

# TABLE OF CONTENTS

PART I

Only one ship is seeking us, a black-
Sailed unfamiliar, towing at her back
A huge and birdless silence. In her wake
No waters breed or break.

—*Philip Larkin*

North of Marysville on route 99,
Butte County
comes back to me

the way landscape does when you're driving alone
reading new road signs
to an old past

and the sad beauty of yellow
sycamores somewhere
between Live Oak and Durham

summons you again, the way landscape
does when fall turns on
its sad charm

and the old town in the old dream
lies just ahead
in the afternoon

sun. I ease by
orchards of thin black arms,
pushing it to sixty,

prune trees
with their white puttee
trunks, their pink haze.

Now this yellow landscape of the moon
with the lava tumors and the wild blue
corn-flowers. Which are rumors? What is true?

I remember the fairgrounds.

I remember driving into town
from Oregon

the first time,
the baby burning with fever,
the streets all named for flowers.

I am dressing pheasants in a lighted gazebo
by an almond orchard on the outskirts of town;
the late autumn dark

surrounds me. I have arranged closed eyes
above my head, five necks inclining like sad clowns
hanging in vines. Soft, the whine of a distant train.

I ease ring-necks from their strange repose,
one by one. Thirty years have passed, and I compose
myself, thrilled by the dead aim

of the mind's eye when the stark
cry rises from the past, the brandy
Labrador staring when the burgundy

breasts rise and rise and rise,
falling and falling. All fall down
we used to cry, our childhood pockets full,

our posies tucked away. Soft, the whirr of a car
on the river road. Indigo, wheat green, gold umber falling
to the yellow fields, retrieve, retrieve,

and the past drops at my feet from the sky.
Burning rice blazes to the east,
orange rolling over the burning sheaves,

the smoke handsome in the far
afternoon, northern California in flames, my hands
full, feathers ruffling in the night, a feast

of colors, the shades of blue-black

green, preening out of the sixties, the land
of dreams, the land of flesh, coming back.

Keeping my journal on the outskirts of a town
I lived in years ago,
adding up the last few days,

I pause to watch the sun go down,
listening to a magpie
quarrel until it plays

out somewhere in the almond orchard below,
black limbs under the pastel sky,
rows of forms above the darkened aisles

of lace-weed green I cannot see. My window
view is screened. I return to the page
with John and Bob and Ben who will not know

I have come back alone
to sit beneath the town square elms without the rage
they loved me by, by day, child hostages grown

and gone, nor that the river bed
changed course and John's orchard sold,
who have no need to be alone,

to drive by one more time the red pistachio trees
in the fall, to walk on crunchy leaves
along the almond rows, to be not dead,

and free. I lay down my pen,
and leave the journal to the sunset and passed time.
Long ago in the high foothills nearby,

my first California fall, I fired a rifle

with my eye so close to the scope
the recoil opened a half moon

on the ridge of my cheekbone.
The scar lingered for years, then was gone.
Now almost everyone's gone. Something about home.

Here in a sun-patch among the redwoods
one day before my homeward
plane, I remember our walks on Hawks Road
to the brook, the way we showed

each other the new fallen hickory
nuts, the shadows where the dog-wary
partridge flew the month before yesterday,
the initials on the old beech tree

grown into script. I remember the vines
dangling down from the old pine
past the turn, and the well where the farm
disappeared, then the long reach down

to the low wooden bridge overflowing with rain.
Our retriever put up the mallard pair again,
brought back sticks you had thrown
across the small pond—our times

in our seasons. On our mile walk home
even the dog picked up the pace, honing
in with a stick or a branch
or a half log balanced in his mouth, prancing

across the wetland road in his personal seasons
past the spring pussy willows
and the ruby red bud in fall,
heady with his own private reasons.

the early morning drive in the dark
gathers the valley fields along the river edge
for keeps, the ridge of Pocumtuck

Mountain closer in the stark
pre-dawn sky; shadows of black
and white cows mark

time in their own ways. We who
are also old school, park
by the new pool and leave the dark

for the blue waters of our morning
laps, marking our own time alone
before the light dawns,

and the drive back home.

*—for Karen and John O'Brien*

The mid-August sheen
of the Vineyard oaks,
motionless, leaf by leaf,
is leather green.

Above the channel lake
where the spear grass wavers
beyond the cottage yard,
in seeming breath-takes,

a white butterfly
hesitates out of the morning blue
and disappears. Who knows
the code of the gull's cry

in a summer scene
of white on green
where everything is background
and time is fog-scrubbed clean?

Whatever is bearing down
has the soft summer touch.
I am all ears
after the plane's drone

is gone. Now I remember
what it was that struck me
loading the dinghy
yesterday in the harbor:

that school of fingerlings
just beneath the surface
scuttled by an underwater surprise:
they were all eyes.

Near the skeletal orchard where the stone wall
turns, we follow our old trail, listening for grouse
in the "Old World" woods beyond our house

where sticky pricker-thistles nag on our sleeves
and beech leaves hang silent as leather:
"This is where I found her,"

rounding the turn where the double prints began
in the silence of the falling December snow
"fourteen years ago."

Upon a scene, upon a time
near tall red oaks in a meandering line
at a crossroads of an animal kind,

a ring of trampled snow, wing beaten, an arena defined
as though angels had bedded down
coupling, and angel arms

in ecstatic flutter quieted of a sudden
in all of nature's providing.
I knelt to touch her

so untouched, then saw the lupine
teeth marks of the clamped wolf jaw
on her rectum.

I dragged the wingless doe
from the miraculous thrashing,
weightless on the new fallen snow

all the way home. Our autumn

road leads higher, to scrub oaks
and a drop-off lookout by a primeval pine

above disheveled boulders where I found canine
droppings before a small cave one spring day.
And one summer below our mountain I saw gray,

loping across a distant field beyond Stillwater Bridge.
We choose the trail through the taller oaks
beneath the curving ridge to Sanford's pond, and home.

All the way home.

Color red above the water where the sumacs flare.
Color our birches yellow and the autumn sky deep blue.
The morning paper says galaxies are colliding out there.

## THOUGHTS BY THE FAMILY GRAVEYARD
## ON OLD SCOTLAND ROAD

Here on this knoll where the garrison house stood
I can see across the fields where the river turns,
and to my right, the fading stones
where geraniums grow, red as blood.

Forty years ago I first walked this plot
thick with briar brambles and sumac,
though the headstones had slid down to the tarmac
and the granite posts gone, like old cars from a car lot.

Down the years the posts squared a neighbor's garden,
and Mrs. Shaw dragged the headstones higher.
Both neighbors are gone, the lines are re-drawn
and the plot draws some of us nearer.

The way the palm fronds brush and sweep in the sun
opens the late afternoon again.
We have just returned
from a boat ride down river from Dalton.
Here on the deck, my port wine glistens.
Upriver, the mountain cliffs define
themselves against the cloudless sky. My son
changes tapes, and Duke Ellington
measures the afternoon calm.
These palm trees give us time. We have come
a long way from the Yangtze River for these soft sounds
where the river turns, and goes on.

The eddies from the downstream tide
make surface swirls around our Marlow dock
on the Hawkesbury River. Tied
to the dock boat cleat, our crab trap locks
a bottom crawler beneath the pocket
bait—a knitted noose of dangling mullet.
He drops from the web ramp like a stalled machine
and joins the waiting game.
Night after night we repeat the same
routine. Out of the water in an empty plastic bucket
he lives for days, alert, ashes black.
Reach into the range of his double claw arc,
he'll take two fingers. In his one kilo suit
he waits inside pure armor, orb-eyed, pure brute.

hangs in long after the outboard motors drop off
the daily workers. Inside the cotton batten, kookaburras sound
off. The white pages of the river are bound
together, the late summer stuff
of weather in Australia, and we wait beneath the arms
of the eucalyptus trees we cannot see.
They will be bare and peeling against the sky come ten
o'clock, our last leisurely
morning at the river. When images appear,
the bend in the river will be before us once again
and rare mangrove openings will beckon
"come." For now, the whiteout gives us what we hear,
a shrimp trawler grinding gears along a far shore,
sea ducks sounding their squabbles somewhere near.

Off the far shore above the channel marker, a white pelican
drifts downstream, stands in the shallows, then swims
up along the mangrove shore. The clouds are higher this morning,
the river mist gathers between the mountains.
A fishing trawler appears upstream trailing gulls
over its rig. Here, crows caw. The first motorboat whirrs
from the public dock a quarter mile away. It is almost fall.
We have come from the other world. All these things occur
before our eyes. The hush of the slight wind through the palms
curls the yellow swords green again, and the sun
rises higher behind the mountains, beyond the clouds. The day
takes on its shape as the light gives and takes away.
This bend in the river is the place we have been given,
our last day at the end of the tourist season.

At this low tide bend in the silver-brown lake
kookaburras jaw in the mangroves.
I have hauled our mud crab traps, and the waves
from a houseboat moving upstream ruffle a slight wake
where they rest on the bottom by the floating dock.
Across the way by the red blinking channel buoy, a boy
leans with his pole from the bow of his anchored boat.
The blue heron stalking our shore beyond the wharf float
has disappeared in the mangroves, and the rain returns. The boy
pulls at his motor and his long metal boat moves downstream.
Through the palm trees before our patio deck, a distant green
light blinks at the public dock. The rain creates pock
marks on the broken river face, passing us by,
watching the moving water under the heavy dark sky.

## PART II

Who's turned us round like this, so that we always,
Do what we may, retain the attitude
Of someone who's departing?

—*Rainer Maria Rilke*

A half-mile in on Mountain Shadow Lane,
Black Angus lounge after a three-day rain.
Here on the deck above clusters of clematis vine
sunflower seeds scatter below the railing tray
where morning colors came and went against the sky.
Beyond the barn a former colonel mows the hay
in sweeping tractor turns before the idling pistons
play against the distant crows conversing one
to one, then two, beyond the field. Now again
the tractor churns the foot high grass to grain.
It is all a matter of time. The peonies have already gone.
Back home my brother's late iris have begun to bloom
on the vacant New Hampshire farm.
Here in northern Virginia, cousins gather in June.

—*for Charles and Barbara Hayward*

Beyond the Manassas ridge
the black Angus cows repair,
eyeing our advance—

we watch them topping off
their stomach bags full. We
are cousins from the North

replacing an old bridge,
musing over old wars,
eyeing the needlework

from old drawers. The Angus,
too, are curious: rheumy-nosed,
huffing air, they stare,

unaware they are like Epicurus
in their diet. Serene
and quiet, they reproduce

themselves. They weigh us
watching them, after hours
among the April flowers.

*—for Charles and Barbara Hayward*

The black stiletto green
of the early evening
hills above the Tiber Valley

stills the distant dog, but he
resumes, and swallows
thrill the chilly air. We

have driven from Rome on our way
north, to play
the old May game another time,

to be exactly here where the murmuring
mountains calm
and the spring irises bloom.

Artichokes, peaches, lettuce—
all purple ripe, for the garden
yearns. What is sown is sown.

Somewhere, just now, beyond
the cypress lines,
a distant chain saw whines.

The patio far above the Tiber shadows
in the late afternoon sun in June
and cicadas grind antennae in the vines
whose yellow tendrils dangle in the wind.
We have driven from Rome knowing
the pinnacle pines were here beyond these stucco
geranium pots and that the cocks would crow
in the distant neighbor's yard as the day winds down.
One fall I picked olives here
in the yard, and we ate the first pressing on fresh bread
at the nearby press. Now new green
BBs bide among the silver sheen.
Along the raised stucco drive, dark red
roses contrast well these olives ever near.

:the mathematics of a hundred
pink flamingoes landing
in an S curve, standing
one legged, gobbling without dread;

the algebra of white
horses born brown, here and there
in the mist where
they stood before, all night;

the calculus of black
fighting bulls beyond fences
doing time; their senses
virginal. They lack

nothing. Here are the essentials,
the late fall shades of Provençal.

we make our picnic on the steep slope field
to watch him tie by hand the sun-
baked hay, and kneel and feel the bundle yield
to his straightening legs and straightening

back. He walks slowly with a ramrod stride
up the soft road to the barn. The wide
valley of the Montafon is green and Sunday
calm. Now she slowly unwraps the hay

from the draped wire and rakes. An aerial tramway
red dots above Schruns
to the hand-gliders' takeoff run:
tiny birds float through the day.

We eat apples and cheese,
doze in the sun. Further up the mountain, daisies
and thistles deepen the view.
There is nothing more we can do

and we start down. Our picnic place
is June clean. The space
we took is gone. No, not a trace.

A reef archipelago in a dream:
I spot a coral Graeco-Roman
head sculpted in curls
of soft moss, marblean.

Attend my aquamarine play,
her pose insists: ponder how serene.
Her sculptor is naval,
centuries old. I float on an arm

of stone, an unruly wave
laps at coral bone.
Inches above the sea she reigns.
Her cheekbones

glisten in the sun,
color her eyes blue-green.
Awake it comes to me that I am she.
Tone is everything.

in a blue sky gale, we pass giant anthills
in the casuarina pines dead still
between the mangroves
and the white waves

gnashing the bleached forearm of Paradise
Beach. The black bulbous tree warts outsize
ten human heads. They raise
their question in their own way.

Our way leads by a path to an abandoned dump
and barking dogs, by a mangrove pond,
by a reach of surf-gnarled stumps
to the other side and a long blonde

beach, serene, without a sound.
Two pelicans patrol the waters before us
as we eat our bread and fruit. The hush
of their dives ends in spreading round

wakes,—collapses  of leather
and feathers rise laconic and arrayed.
Our Crusoe beach is weather
born, pristine. This hour, we keep away

the gale. Walking home through the pines
we find a lovely black stone.
The fire at the Bimini Bay dump is burning.
On our bay front dock you say the tide is turning.

In the courtyard of the Napoleon
House, we sit around a black iron
table remembering Stony and Sparrow
and their room above the narrow
curving stairs, off the balcony
above the potted palms and geraniums,
two streets over from Bourbon
where in the sixties the Bayou Room
rocked with Stoneback.
When part of the country died with Jack,
Stony made another pact
with art, this time with books,
and went on the road to Kentucky
and Red Warren, and the new old
South. We have just come from 420 Bourbon
where the Bayou Room,
unpainted, appears long ago sold.
Now "Crawdaddies," it offers souvenirs
of a new New Orleans.

Behind St. Louis Cathedral Square
in the house where Faulkner
wrote Soldiers Pay, a poetry bookstore
brightens Pirates Alley. We're headed there
now with Stony's poems,
almost forty years of lines
unwinding, sounding from songs
into song.

*—For Stony and Sparrow*

We eased into a plotter's maze of tree-named lanes
in Yonkers on a cold and showery day,
windows down in our melon-colored compact Ford,
wary of Canada geese flat-footing in their private rainy ways,

stealthing by headstones talking to themselves
the way honkers take note with guttural precisions.
We drove along Elm, cut across Pine, decisions
hedged by memory; we were looking for Catalpa.

On the border of Laurel and Ivy, just across from Crown Grove,
we found that strange blank page of stone
and parked. A black squirrel, no longer alone,
headed off toward Beech. Those before us left pennies,

a small clam shell, a now soggy poster "from our class."
Someone had tucked a ticket stub under a rock, from a Williamstown
playhouse, from Arthur Miller's *All Our Sons*.
Standing there landlocked in Woodlawn, near the Hudson,

we took to ourselves the vast oak overhead, overspreading,
and the open ocean beneath our feet where Ishmael drifts.
Some books shape the mind's dream like a phantom drawing.
As we opened the car, a crow jumped from an overhead pine, cawing.

*—for Robin Gajdusek*

Robins brush spring landscapes in war-weary zones,
Old wounds olive-orange in fugitive tones
Becoming lines. Memory recapitulates that old front
In a hedgerow glade three nights,
Now shutter shades of the timeless hunt
Gone wrong. Reversal's irony occurs in another light,
A stranger one where memory filters fugitive days
Juxtaposing seasons of the past with real night sounds
Designed to loan us back our primal wounds,
Until the actual landscape re-appears where he lay
Still, the enemy dream all around,
Eden in Normandy, pitch black,
Keeping him safe, bleeding in the dark.

When all was said and done, he left Paris
for the last time, his love affair reborn
for the last time, Shakespeare & Company packed
to the gills, his poems on the wing buffeting Notre Dame
and his plane climbing toward  home for the last time,
leaving Lucky Lindy below forever landing at Orly
for the last time, his old Normandy landing at Omaha
and the long nights in the Gravelotte hedgerows alone
when the Conqueror bound up his wounds for the last
time, on the wing toward home and the early
California sun, home, minutes north of the Golden
Gate, pondering that old gypsy Pilar
studying his palm, tracing the crack.
Soon he would sleep, the curtain falling on the final act.

The fact that fall accounts
for spring and its ways, calls us
in the interim to celebrate the soft and quiet circus
of early summer, the way iris
picks up where forsythia leaves off, then roses
unfold until the maples blaze.
We recognize the nature of things that count
the days.
The perfect destroyers in the air call us
to the perfect blooms
that summer spreads before us
on our table in this green room
between the hills we call our own.
Surely goodness and mercy meet in the ease
of change when flowers blaze beneath the wings of bees.

—*for Gene and Stan Koehler on their 50<sup>th</sup>*

Here on this mountain rim
before the silver-tarnished sea
and the gathering wind, we
raise our glasses once again

to the clearest sentences of trust
we know by heart, our ritual
of say and dance, the old millennial
sacrament that binds us, dust

to dust. This mountain rim
before the silver-tarnished sea
is ours now, the redwood trees
below, this very edge of the brim

of our mornings and afternoons together.
This landscape holds us in our time,
these roses we wear, these words we rhyme,
this mountain grass, the lovely Heather.

*—For Heather and Julian*

in Shanghai down the dark street from the hotel
after the fatso panda peddled the ball
in the air and the child acrobats sailed
from the ceiling swings tweezing and the hip models
in high heels and slit gowns
walked the line to "Stomping at the Ritz":

in the darkness, the rail
is hip-high iron, warm to my hand's Braille.
Xiao Chun smiles
words that keep us
to ourselves. Our talk is simple
and we laugh. Once she asked, playing the fool,

what is a perfect body? and the logic of her double
question gives me a bridge from a childhood dream
to a broken body whole.
Overhead, night carp are swimming.

we speed thirty-five miles
an hour and the driver will not be responsible
for our cameras if we take Mao almost smiling
in his Mausoleum photograph before the aisles

of troop trucks and the lonely standing boys with gun barrels
pointing at the sky across their breasts, and pull
over at the gate to the Forbidden City, tall
and red and everything the movie Last Emperor tells

except the square with the five thousand Buddhist monks
and the grass growing seedy in the cracks between the chunks
of courtyard stones: soldiers on R and R now filing
into the empty court smiling,

teenage boys squatting into regiments of quail
in soft brown uniforms, happy below the bullhorn's call
to their regimental colors and their Colonel's
stare toward the General's air of non-committal,

observant nonchalance. Soon five thousand soldiers fill
the square and file in a double-column hustle
past the jade black turtle and the gilded bronze unicorn
through the Hall of Supreme Harmony, and then they're gone.

PART III

They clear the creeping moss—
Elders and juniors—aye,
Making the pathways neat
        And the garden gay;
And they build a shady seat . . .
        Ah no, the years, the years;
See the white storm-birds wing across!

        —*Thomas Hardy*

I caught alewives
with my hands
in the concrete troughs
easing Lily Pond down

to the Saugus River,
and spread them
on the grass like knives
glistening in the sun

glistening in the kitchen light
on Saturday night
spread headless on the Lynn Item
bones and soft-flesh

in the photograph,
knuckles on the trough slime
finger touch, the brush
of tail, the rush

of shadows gone.

I walked the way to Stackpole Field
from Lynnhurst hill,
and sat in the stadium
watching them play,
the boys with the pigskin ball,
when I was ten,
Buddy and me and Sonny Adrien.

We sat in the stadium
high and gray
on Saturday,
and the sachem headdress
shone in the sun
when I was ten
in Saugus town.

Shoulder pads crackled,
the ball sailed on air
when I was ten
in a wooden stadium
by a pond,
through the woods,
down Elm, up Appleton.

I watched through a dream,
going out for the team,
while the sun curled the leaves
on the trees,
and they fell
all fall, every fall,
and I was fourteen.

I walked the way to Stackpole Field
after school every day,
with Jim, in the fall,
old names in the air,

fame in the air,
up Central, down Main,
then Summer.

I walked the ways of childhood sun
and childhood rain,
folded in an album.
Doug Waybright so fair,
Doug Waybright so blonde, so dead.
Across from the stadium,
they drained Lily Pond.

I walked the ways to Stackpole stadium
when Lynnhurst fields led on to fields.
I dressed for the game
when Summer Street was always fall.
We ran after it all
in Eden, that old park.
We scrimmaged our fall days into dark.

*—for John Burns*

blue, working her brush back
and forth; skeins
of blue silk unravel into the sun-slaked
pines: her shadow
glistens on the planks' blue

veins: done and done
and done; she dips, smoothes
her shadow into the sun: her nurse-rhyme
sounding in her head: now
for my half-sister dead, now

for my grandmother's bed. The tiger maples
blossom over the rail, over the girl-child
watching through her knees, watching
the blue lake shadow
frieze: done unto thee, done

unto me; she paints the sun deck
blue in June and the sun
deck blazes in the sun: fair
is fair. Blue water, blue
skies, oh flowing hair.

she embraces her marriage
for what it is, and defies
the wind. Her carriage
is her special armor: it belies

the rawness of edges
underneath. Only she knows
what she knows. She hedges
only at the final step. Snow

melts on another beach. Now
she steps again in sand,
smiles at a row
of gulls edging sideways

like a wedding band.

sentences darken her white pad.
she minds herself and the words
tell her what she knows. White shad
sparkle in the waters of her prose.

At her glass top desk she composes
over layers of clear tone: her life,
her style. Once eight roses
shadowed her pen in another life.

the library's high sunset
mirrors the glinting hoods at their feet,
the mallard's laugh, the wet
depths of the brain's deepest book. Concrete

steps rise toward the glass
doors and the beech tree bares
its breast. Fingertips pass
the knife. Her yellow braid flares.

and a rose falls
from the opened page,
the curled edge
saying how the red syllables

broke. She is taken again
by the screech
of the gull within arm's reach
hovering over her pen

on the Costa del Sol. She hears
the silence. She knows
the sound. Inside her hair
red petals fall, but nothing shows.

and turbans her scarf
on a winter Delaware beach, tracing
the faded prints beside husband and son,

hearing the water break and the ocean
secrets talk, knowing that jetsam
turns to words. She walks the January

sand, watches the edges
move, tosses two blue
stones and the hopscotch blurs: oh Mary

Mary. The boy runs
to flush a tern, spread-eagles,
never looks back until she's flying.

and the Connecticut Valley
is down there: I point
this and that where, we laugh
and watch the last light fade

over the Berkshires. You say the first
South Deerfield lights spread
our buffet. I have brought
Muscadet. The night blue tinges
the wine with a reminiscence

of bouquet. The first evening plane
crosses the sky without a sound. You
unwrap cellophane
from a half-sandwich, slightly
squashed: peanut butter on wheat. If

I'm going to drink, I have
to eat, you laugh: we are the only ones
who know we're on this soapstone hill
with fetching pails and tumbled
crowns until the Ranger's headlights

flare. We edge down the spiral
stairs. At Foster's in Greenfield
we buy broccoli and lobsters
and firm yellow pears.

Blue bay, black crow, shadow
spruce: the way the low
gliding gull settles
on the low tide meadow

(black rockweed yellowing)
wing lilting, feet first,
underscores the tolling bell
from the southwest, bellowing

faintly from Long Island Plantation
(mid-channel buoy
or Sunday summoning) in the lee
of my August imagination:

the wing-still white descent,
the unseeming search
for the solitary perch,
the unplanned, imminent, re-ascent.

in late afternoon appear
in dooryards, browsing
the high mid-summer
grass. They lift and lower

their heads, musing.

At high noon, the harbor mackerel
slash in schools
at the steel
jig, flashing.

and shove off, their raucous
morning caucus
now above deep spruce,
loose

as leads on a thrown net:
now set
in the dark place. Moving, they resume
their off-tune

talk onshore. In the rockweed, a mink
slinks
the morning further on, and disappears.
Here

and there a cormorant gawks and dives, his black
shadow track
now gone in the incoming tide, glistening.
I am listening.

So there was my daughter with no strings attached
flop-bowing from the waist,
her jacket patched,
bringing down the house
three thousand miles from home.

Seattle, the city of rainy weather
and dance. Her fellow puppet is Heather.
They are clearly in this together,
here on the boards in Imperial Russia
outwitting the Czar

(who, she reads, is wary of violence and forbids
boxing matches).

Petrushka wakes up
and plays on his notions
around a dresser and its drawers.
He goes through the motions.
He pulls no punches. He pulls no strings.

He makes the most of it
while the stage hands in the wings
wind the window panel, center back wall.
Colors, then stars rise and fall
on wires in chronometric precision.

So how could a real earthquake fit into a dance
three minutes before passion awakens?
Remember, first-nighters and all you czars,
the earth is moving,
all art is time.

Puppets always slip a czar's noose
when everything cuts loose.

The outside petals of the rose
darken the top of a long stem
inclining dry blood, the still life pose
above the table's stories, the invisible mayhem

of time. Outside, the afternoon
sky deepens the chestnut leaves
with the barest tint of harvest moon.
Sun softens the balcony eaves.

The sentinel poise of the fading rose
quickens its leaves of curls,
its brown-red thorns exposed
above pears shouldering dark grape pearls

bunched to form a crown
of ripeness by a gold-tipped glass
half-filled with wine.

## PART IV

The masts go white slow, as light, like dew, from darkness
Condensed on them, on oiled wood, on metal. Dew whitens in darkness.
I lie in my bed and think how, in darkness, the masts go white.

—*Robert Penn Warren*

On this late morning in late June
two yellow butterflies traverse the beach peas
where the seawall begins.
Mourning doves sound in the air. I can see

Long Island Plantation, darker blue above the sun glare
sea, behind the closer Sister Island's darker green,
beyond the tide rip glaze, that intermittent creamy
mid-tide roil off Red Point's hogback shore.

We have come again to our tidal cove
of greens and blues. One poplar remains
among our shoreline spruce; its leaves
from my childhood story book flutter like coins.

Our last son at home is in China, on his way
to Shanxi to see the Buddhist shrines
color the hills. Here, a nearby birch divides like a tuning
fork before me, beyond my reach, just out of play.

Sitting on the deck away from the mid-morning sun,
reading Mary Oliver on Whitman, I hear the bulkhead windows
of the house begin to open
downward, one by one, and I know

Kaimei is letting in the sun-fogged Sunday
morning air of this island coast. She
has returned from a long walk with the dog, and now
can hear the high tide lapping of the beach

stones as she works her way through
the preface to her teenage countryside life
in China. We have been to the Odd Fellows
Hall for breakfast with the summer clientele. My wife

and I. That rhyme in my late years seems right,
irregular but sound, akin to these deciduous larch
trees, still conifer to the bone though bare in March
before the yellow purple buds begin to form, bright

with spring: hackmatack, tamarack,
from the Montana forests above Kalispell
of my youth, to the Maine woods. Sounds tell
us more than we know: the wavelets on the rocks,

ducks softly squawking among the rockweed,
wind in the birches waving
arms across the darker spruce, the lone gull whispering
overhead, scanning the sea for her daily bread.

Early morning after the rain, the range
of blues and greens retains the dark night's
rainbow dream. Black cormorants in flight
from nowhere hurry singly by, and the strange

vibrato of crows lifts from the woods. I
remember little of the night except a fragment
of the long playing childhood dream, a long lost tent
opening beside a river, then closing, as if a great eye

blinked, and birches swaying in the sun
in full yellow Nod, that land of early summer play,
the way it recapitulates itself here in the early light of day
while diamond water sparkles blindingly East beneath the sun

and a lone lobster boat negotiates into the blazing light
and disappears. Yet the lingering engine hums
until the wind in the trees is the only sound, then
the crows again, nearer, slightly frenzied, still out of sight.

The intermittent sun glare from the boat hauling traps
off the Plantation shore measures the high gaps
in the cirro-cumulus clouds slowly moving east,
though the barely perceptible breeze off the water comes back west,

with its fresh morning smell. The tops of the shore spruce
are sentinel-still, fathomable only to the garrulous
crows who abide momentarily on their serious
migration deeper into the woods. Whatever truce

they reach is private, unrelated to the crosswinds
of July. I too accept the calm between,
crow-like in my own way, beneath the high easterly scene
of cotton tinged with blue and the salt cool breeze. I find

this surface scene as laden with mystery and certitude
as last night's dream where I found myself
in a turbulent land before a way home appeared. The shelf
of clouds drifts east; two dolphins cut the surface of this morning mood.

I remember writing "1937" on my multiplication table
papers in Miss Reynolds' room in my yellow Lynnhurst
school, when seventy-two seemed as high as numbers were able
to reach; then weekly the twelfth numeral burst

until a hundred and forty-four seemed sufficient
for all the problems of life. Before I left that yellow school
Miss Bridgham eased me into third percentage
and the mysteries of higher math, and I was ready to travel

the bus to junior high and the world. All
my math teachers now are dead, but the calculus of memory
brings back the names as quickly as I begin to call
the roll: Misters Rice, Lahey, Watson, Haley,

and Miss Fox. They taught me more than what to count.
They taught me special days and how to give
the simple numbers meaning: how they all mount
up, one by one. Addition shows us how to live.

The brush pile on the ledges before our cove
grows higher day by day, as I clear last autumn's
leveled spruce before the coming summer rain.
It looms as background to high grass before the heavy

morning fog. Even as the hidden sun arcs
higher in its morning burn, the sea remains
opaque, as if a sheet of gray has dropped behind
the quiet birches and the sleepless poplar coins. Dark

shadows in the shoreline spruce paint chiaroscuro
depths above the line where further islands yesterday
defined perspective in a different way,
with miles between, then nothing above and everything below

the surface of the Gulf of Maine. Now the first line
of random lobster  buoys dots gray water as the fog
recedes, and overhead the first blue openings appear. Only time
remains before the idea of the sea is clear, even unto Spain.

The morning breakers duplicate themselves with soft rolling ease
and the sun dries the dew on the deck. The cold snap
is over, and the distant water haze
evaporates like disappearing gauze.

Only the sounds of the half-tide waves
resound with the morning calm.
We have just put down the phone
to China where our son has climbed Tai Shan.

Now the outer island fog returns.
The scraggly tops of spruce define
the Sister Island trees that curve above the cotton line.
An oil barge shadows along the bottom edge of white

and disappears across the mid-tide rip. Its engines
hum beyond Red Point and seem to stop. Again
the fog recedes, and the half-summer game goes on.
A familiar family of ducks rides the breakers like a dream.

We have gathered rockweed from yesterday's high waves
and spread it in the sun between the poplar and the deck
to dry for our garden at home, a myriad soufflé
of yellow rubber curls, purple moss and mussels yanked

by the hair from the tide pool floor. From the deck, I
watch the tidal clock tick minor wave by wave,
whitening the basin channels. Two gulls like barrel staves
bob in the rising rockweed soup, eyeing

through water glass the rainbow bottom we have walked
within the hour. They peck and squabble with an underwater life
we cannot see. Their aim is deadly and the end foregone. Brief
summer interludes reveal the private ways we find relief.

Black seaweed laced with yellow drapes
the boulders disappearing in the tide,
and island roses overflow the deck,
their yellow centers candy to the bees that check
each one by one. Pink blossoms ride
the wind, calming between gusts, and gape
again at the afternoon sun, as if July
could multiply the yellow summer days
of late middle age, Eden cast adrift for good,
the dead reckoning stare through the invisible hood
of days to come, as if July might simply stay.
The yellow on the birch leaves is the other story.
They sway and ruffle in the ocean breeze.
Come fall they'll droop, ready for the winter freeze.

The gull in the fog watches the tide cove fill.
The outline of his breast against the grayer white
matches the froth of the wavelets breaking into the still
scene beneath his ledge. I cannot see beyond him into the bright

mist where two lobster boats work their lines
of traps, growling buoy to buoy. Occasionally
he flaps twice to the rising rockweed at the seawall
edge and bobs among the yellow soup. When he returns

to the ledge he seems to stare beyond the scene.
When the first wave breaks across his feet he lifts again
to the gentle shoreline calm. Closer now, I can discern
his gray wings tinged with black, his yellow beak. When

he dips straight down, his patience pays off. The boats have gone.
His old ledge has disappeared. The cove is calm.

The fifth day of fog breaks on our eastern shore
in the stillness of our mid-summer
stay, and a lone orange buoy floats on the edge
of white, ninety yards out from our ledge.

Our morning view is a study in onshore black and green
as the sun lifts higher above the fog. Dew glistens
on the undersides of thin birch arms
and in the tamarack fur. A passing gull returns

and banks on a dime to crash the tidal soup
where the seaweed rises from its ropey
curls and floats in yellow fronds. As diamonds bead
the rising cove, the whitest blue appears overhead.

overflowing on the deck
make more poignant the spruce
railings aging under the seasonal suns.
They belie their own brown
underside, their southeast bruise flecked
with twigs, and lounge in loose
array seven boards deep,
barely murmuring in the summer wind
as the summer bees flaunt
their carefree summer binge. I want
some distant day, because we cannot keep
the dearest things, to find
at least in some forgotten drawer
this barest hint of what we knew was more.

Wild roses, overlapping the edge of the deck,
have lost their blooms, and a lone bee moves in vain
from rose-hip to hip the size of peas flecked
with blush, the first traces of Maine's

second rose blossoms, sunset red, round
as giant marbles, stem-sheathed in green-fanged
Asian stars. For now, swelling without a sound,
the bush is shadow green and black. The faint clang

of the Sunken Money Ledge buoy tolls
the near-end of summer, and the near beach
peas have turned half brown. As the tide rolls
softly in, a gull swoops by, his soft screech

hanging in the air, then once again the late
summer silence of yearning, lifting again that old weight.

Fog webs whiten the young shore larch,
green moss stubble-beards the trunks of spruce
looming with their higher dark. Our sky-gray
tide pond merges with the mist, silently swallowing

the shadow outer ledge. When the snapping blaze
of our softwood fire turns our gaze inside, we follow
the random trail of things that clear days
overlook, when the outer view is green

islands and a tacking sail. Here's that round clay
water jug from Gredos, Spain; the wine glass from Bonn;
the yellow-blue tablecloth—St. Maries de la Mer;
the Xi'an terra cotta warrior calendar;

the round black buoy from Scotland's own east
coast. Those days come clear in the fog's white yeast.

In the dead still silence of the low tide morning
fog, a white web reveals its interlocking frames
in knit-spun space between the green
spine ends of new growth spruce, suspension

firm, delicately twined, sky-white against the brown
late summer grass, its oblong center lace defined
by space and emanating stairs of ladder lines,
Parcheesi-like, expanding outward like a fern.

It seems to drift in air, yet holds its own
by thongs known only to its absent queen
somewhere nearby in a darker arm
of fate, waiting for the sun to warm

her woven lair. She has the time.
Nothing flies in the morning air. The fog hangs in.

By eight o'clock the sun is shore-spruce high
and the low tide pool mirrors the low
eastern sky, white with offshore fog.
Overhead, the cloudless onshore sky

is coloring-book blue. A lobsterman I know,
his stern sail set, hooks his toggle
buoy and wraps the trap line in the pulley
groove. His boat growls slowly in an arc

and the trap appears. I know his ritual by heart.
When he waves and disappears around the point, surely
clear days and foul will follow him home. I mark
the buoy where he has moved his trap. The black

toggle sits almost motionless on the slow
wake of the tide, six fathoms over the box below.

The eastern sky is dark after last night's rain
and the low cloud sun silvers the bay on a line
toward the Duck Island Light, still hidden within
the offshore storm. The morning breeze quickens

a silver change from gray to black, and the horizon
is a sudden knife of light. No human hand could mine
this scene; only the inner eye that knows the sun
in its rising. Overhead the clouds from the west

open blue gaps, and shore birches glisten
in their moist yellow-green. These island vestments
shine after the rain like some human preening.
without guile, an innocence so natural it seems

more than it is. Our August landscape
assumes a clarifying tone in its hourly changing shape.

Soft white rollers unravel from the afternoon blue
half tide, and the sun brightens the rainbow
buoys between our inlet cove and the fog glow
of the nearer Sister shore. Thick gray glue

seals off the further view. Our childhood guests have gone.
Rollers wash our boulder beach. Soon
the sea-change begins again, as western
clouds loom overhead and the steel sea darkens

beneath the bobbing buoys. What plays out
before our eyes has all played out before,
yet it is more than a changing tidal shore.
It is the past itself and those lone buoys without

lines drifting un-retrieved on that other sea
we visit in dreams, and occasionally in our memory.

*—for Roger and Lyn*

PART V

The old barn at the bottom of the fogs.
Its only windows were the crevices
All up and down it.

—*Robert Frost*

*—anonymous  (c. 1120 BCE, China)*

That white cloud in the sky
becomes a hill, then a person.
The road goes miles into the distance.
Mountains and a river divide us.
Please don't die.
I am still wishing you may come.

—*Wang Wei*  (*701-761, T'ang Dynasty*)

Late sunlight deepens the market village.
The thicket path bulges with cattle and sheep
wending home. An old peasant watches for his shepherd
son, leans on his staff, waits at his gnarled wood
gate. A pheasant cries in the new wheat.
The silk worms are sleeping. Only a few mulberry leaves keep.
Men from the fields, still shouldering their hoes,
stop to talk. They visit a long time, then longer.
This is the place. I envy their dallying and their easy ways.
I have a sorrow. I sing the old song of "Shih-wei."

*—Tu Ch'iu  (c. 800-850, T'ang Dynasty)*

You better not lay it all on money and that coat.
I tell you, grab the first minutes—you have them now.
If pretty flowers interest you, pluck them. Do it quickly.
Hesitate and nothing ripens. Why break twigs later?

—*Wang Wei* (*701-761, T'ang Dynasty*)

I am pushed to the boulder by the rising stream
and the weeping willows brush my cup of wine.
Who knows if the spring breeze feels my ideas?
Why else this blowing, these petals here, and here.

—*Su Tung-p'o* (*960-1279, Sung Dynasty*)

Our rice fields ripen too late.
We eye the fields for frost. What
wind will bring the freeze? Rain drenches
everything. The harrow heads grow green. Sickles rust.
My eyes are cried out—now more rain.
Our lovely rice stalks yellow the green mud.
We camp a month on the banking,
harvesting under clear skies, following the wagon home,
sweating, shoulder dead, hauling to market.
The price is a giveaway: bran chaff.
Our cow pays for taxes. Our roof fires the stove.
Planning is useless. Next year we'll starve.
The authorities demand cash because the rice is worthless.
The Northwest Border invites the Tangut hordes.
Big minds fill the court. People are in strife.
Yes, I envy the River Lord's wife.

—*Lhesa Ukraina*

Stop looking at the moon, you know that it's spring.
The moon watches—he wants to know things
and he listens on the sly.
He has seen us before
and he's heard you say those words. I
wonder if you mind forgetting.
You musn't look at the moon in spring.

You musn't look at the weeping willow.
Sorrow vines
hang down with other times,
drooping with a hurt of fire,
lines that burned us once before.
I wonder if you mind forgetting.
Stop looking at the weeping willow.

—*translated with Svetlana Voitiuk*

—*Taras Shevchenko*

Trailing the sun, a cloud
unfolds its red lapels,
beckons the sun to fall
asleep into the sea blue shroud
of roses and mist
as a child would.
Our eyes shine in this image
of the smallest turning page
of time, as a heart quiets,
knowing the Shepherd is at hand.

Our assailant, the mist
shrouds the sea
and the amethyst cloud;
darkness beyond the dark
lays a gray fog, stark
and dumb, the sepulchre of the soul.
We do not know where to go
to find another place that is ours,
and we wait for the light as a child
waits for her mother.

—*translated with Svetlana Voitiuk*

—*Taras Shevchenko*

The wind is talking to a copse
of trees, whispering to the tiniest birch,
and a boat floats on the Danube,
solitary in its water fugue.
The boat is on
the water with no one
to stop it or slow it down;
its fisherman is gone.

The boat is floating out to sea
and begins to play
where gigantic swells roll free
and banish every chip caught in their melee,
too far for an orphan boat
in the open sea—
for a wanderer by a foreign copse of trees
to pass despair.

Good people play
the same way freezing waves play.
They look at each other
as the orphan wanderer weeps. Someone
asks where the orphan has gone,
but no one has heard a thing. Or seen a thing.

*translated with Svetlana Voitiuk*

PART VI

—we study the shadows of bird's wings and of leaves,
we listen for inaudible sounds, we retrace our steps,
we enter the temple on tiptoe at nightfall. . . .

—*Yannis Rítsos*

*1. Rainy Season*

The white butterfly between me
and the top of my ninety nine stairs
down, jump-starts the heavy air
of afternoon. I can see

three ships in the spring
mist, crickets sleeping
through meadow dew, antennae
anchored in old Amoy.

White peony petal, flitting
out of my nap dream, gone
into the green fur peaches. It
returns and goes, clean as bone.

*2. Mist on the Mountain*

and these rowers on the campus lake
take turns drifting;
bird boaters contemplate
the fisherwoman lifting

her empty net, beating the far shore
with a bamboo pole.
The rowers imitate each other's
leisure. In a little while, her net is full.

*3. The White Goat in the Light Rain*

Here above the Buddhist temple, I see
harbor ships coming and leaving, day

after day. They blow great horns
on the move. One ship stays
through the rainy

season; its anchor lights go on
at dusk and glow through the night.
One day in April, I study
the ship closer from the crowded shore,
no one in sight.

The anchor chain is algae
green, the water line is rust.
At the bottom of my mountain, rain
begins and deepens the darkening green.
Massive boulders hover over me in the mist.

Once I stood on one at dawn,
looking beyond the harbor toward Taiwan,
its elephant back spread like a ballroom.
Now this white goat up there in the rain
again, standing as if unseen.

I read and write on our apartment balcony in Beijing,
and inside you are remembering,
and then there are twilight swallows feeding
above the neighborhood poplars, between the stars,

the countryside years gone, Heilongjiang,
teenage years in the fields,
comrades in the fields, swallows
feeding,

so we return to Military Farm #85, north of You Yi,
and the peasants swarm you like honey.
You stand between the green rows where once you kneeled
into the nights, the building

where you raised chickens gone,
the dormitory where you slept. You say
the soil was never dirty for you. You loved
the black earth.

You never saw the white poppies blooming
but you girdled the green fruit so,
and gathered the cream tears
in their season, entrusted with the key

by the Party. Our best photo
shows you standing alone in an ochre muddy road
leading to the horizon, poplars
on both sides getting smaller and smaller,

holding a Kongfu wine bottle
with a pumpkin flower. Later,
we fill the bottle with that black earth
and carry it to the other side of the world.

—what of the fields we battled into the summer
nights, weeding,
so soon from home
to borderland spies disappearing on the hill,
feeding the winter moon,

so soon the black fields green, yellow
fields white, bags of grain threshing,
corn, soy beans, snow,
spies who were never there,
dreaming on our long brick oven

beds, what of the fields, battling
into the autumn dark, bundles, stacks,
early snow piling, our peasant
killing his dog to surprise us with delicacies,
we were all eyes

for tracer bullets on the prairie
at New Year's,
our abandoned dumplings gelling
into soup, quelling our winter
play, and what of reverie,—

chopping irrigation ditches past sundown,
urine ice piling, melting into seasons,
opium poppies under the sun,
years of countryside days,
black fields, yellow corn, snow,

the pure school of Mao,
how we learned,

how we yearned for home,
what of those battles and our young red shields,
what of the colors of China's fields?

I saw an old man flying a kite
in Tiananmen Square at six in the morning, the long
line to his paper eagle slung in its clean arc
above Mao's tomb, the People's Congress, the Revolutionary Museum,
and the Forbidden City, a month before Hong Kong
returns to China, and the opium
deal is finished. The early risers own
the square. The old man
minds his business, his eagle stark
against the morning blue, in broad daylight,

the feel of it on his wrist, the feel of it
there in the sky, flying. Kaimei had seen it
all before in a different light, different Mays,
the same ten thousand paper kites flying
as if there were no strings attached, and the days
followed on days. She walked us to the countdown
clock and we counted down. Later, across town
where the Red Guards fought each other, vying
for the radio station where her mother was under house arrest
at the Mechanical Engineering College for being a Capitalist

Roader, she told me how, charge after charge failing,
a young woman ripped off her shirt with five boys trailing
and stormed the parting lines, naked to the waist,
to rout the control room and grab the broadcast
speakers.

From the Ya Lu Zang Bu valley, we must have seemed
a disappearing tree moth, our 1930s bus on the cutback
mountain road to the pass, on the edge of fifteen
thousand feet, leaving the grazing yaks below the whiteout,

pressing our wild blue daisy between the blank pages
of our book, closing and opening, to spread
Yang Zor Lun Lake below us, sandy-shored,
opaline, then Tibetan blue. We were nine

hours from Rikeza on the Red Army road,
hogging the back seat of the bus
with no shock absorbers, holding on,
our heads full of valley rapeseed fields

as yellow as our old first grade play pegs,
rainbow women bending in the sun, sparkling
child eyes black enough to break one's heart,
white ribbon flags ragged on fence posts,

tree poles, window sticks. Description
is the weakest tale of passion. Memory
betrays the color of the sky. The next night back in Lhasa,
two lower lights burned in the palace Budala.

The yellow hardwood fire deepens to red
coals quivering in their dying. Rain
lashes the roof, and the seaward
windows glisten where the lampshade shines,
black mirrors from the whiplash sea.
Your eight foot Chinese curtains frame the night:
silk pandas eating green and blue bamboo.
The rain-blotched windows gleam like pearls we
bargained for in Fujian, the island of Gulang-yu.
You're upstairs, downstairs, everywhere gone from sight.
This afternoon I shot a duck in the rain
and lost my hat in the wind as the tide pulled the floating
body out to sea. I watched it gain
momentum as it reached the rip between
the Sisters and Red Point, a lifeless mote.

In Denver, I leave the Saturday games behind
and walk down Fourth to the presidential street signs
of my boy New England neighborhood, past Harrison
and Garfield all the way west to Colorado—
here, where the late fall turns me around again—
thirty-five years—looking down from a plane,
losing that old California campaign, that old lost cause
of the sixties, our second childhood glow
that dimmed but still moon-lit those middle years
we stayed beyond class in that newer public school
where finalities cannot salve ambition's fears.
The eyes of squirrels overhead are black blazing gauze.
I have walked down Cleveland from the Lynnhurst School
to remind my friend I love him, and to celebrate this pause.

Mt. Etna rises in a long ascent to its broken
top where wisps of smoke disappear in the haze.
It sprawls on its island in a perfect calm.
Driving to Siracusa today, where the blaze
of postcard eruptions turned our heads,
we edged at great speed around its feet,
watching its absolute presence spread
until our circumvention ended where the highways meet
and we turned toward Archimedes' tomb
and Heiron's altar where the throats
of four hundred bulls once gushed on a stone loom
of blood, the final weaving only a footnote
to ancient faith. Now the breeze has died
and the Sea spreads again before Etna as his bride.

Among the six anchored sloops below, one yawl
rocks almost imperceptively in the cerulean
calm. We have come from the ruins of Hera's temple
in Agrigento where the northern colonnade
encloses its architrave still, in the Sicilian
sun a long walk up the hill
by the prickly pear cactuses and the olive
trees. We rested in the shade, our camera full
of the perfect Doric Temple of Concord below,
and below that the eight columns of Heracles,
the oldest temple dedicated to the hero belonging
to the Romans and the Greeks. The shore below
belongs to us; its waters clarify
our journey there and here, this lull
in a fortnight colloquy of travels
with our son who grows each day beyond us, taller
and in other simple ways. The yawl has hauled
its anchor and is moving on, trailing
the slightest froth of white in its final
wake.

in the Turtle River, his soft spoken deck
leans almost over the sloping bank, the morning
after the second October snow, the dark
stream mirror-white, then dark again,
coming and going  at this crowded turn where the brown
leaves of the green ash and the basswood join
in a watercolor stained with fall. The high
further slope is strewn with trunks and limbs,
stark against the snow where for many lines
a white tail doe has browsed the bank,
pausing and lifting to study the eyes
she cannot see that watch her. Her page is blank
as she stares, and she resumes her random
meal. When he returns she will be gone.

The late October North Dakota mid-morning sun
is halving the fire-engine red geranium
blossom leaning over the tops of books
disorderly arranged in rows and stacks
that seem to elevate the purity of hues
so intricate in hexametric views
designed to blaze as midnight horizon fire,
a red that belies the subtleties of the spectrum pyre.
As the elevating sun re-designs its shifting gaze,
a small cactus across the room ignites a bloodspot blaze.
Our geranium, now left to lean
above the tomes toward tomorrow's sun
still celebrates the sunless blazing red,
lifting its morning moonlight blossom head.

Something goes with him across the fields
as the seasons turn,

something at first in Massachusetts
and Maine, something to do with glades
and old meadows in the sun,

the old poetical lea (from the German *loh,*
as in Waterloo) meaning "grassy field,"

but something also in the other lee,
the quiet in the middle of the storm, rocking
alone on a childhood porch in the lightning

gale, standing alone in the bow of the rising
and falling transport ship

heading into the dark of Europe;
something goes with him in the war
and in the peace, in Iowa and Boston,

in the corner of the field where the deer
stands at dusk, where the markers

shield the dark from the names, deeper
than Scotland and Denmark, this keeper
of the fields, tender

in his care, steady in his touch, something
goes with him from the start.

He knows the long walk home through the woods by heart.

## ABOUT THE TITLE

"Sometimes in summer there are days when the restlessness of the tides and the fearful cold of the sea water and the incessant wind that blows across the afternoon and into the evening make me wish for the placidity of [the] lake in the woods."

—*E.B. White*

DONALD JUNKINS is the most recent winner of the *New Letters* poetry award, and has been the recipient of two National Endowment for the Arts grants. His poems have appeared in nine anthologies including *American Anthology/2* (selected by Anne Sexton) and *The New Yorker Book of Poems*. Major reviews of his poems have appeared in *The Georgia Review, The Sewanee Review,* and *The New York Times Book Review*. Junkins' translation of Euripides' *Andromache* appears in the *Penn Greek Drama Series,* and he translated with Amiya Chakravarty, *A Tagore Reader*. His own poems have been translated into French, Ukrainian, and Chinese. He lives in Deerfield, Massachusetts with his wife, Kaimei Zheng, with whom he has translated a volume of Li Bai's (Li Po) poems. His sixteen line definition of a New Englander appears in John Murray's *A Gentleman Publisher's Commonplace Book*. Junkins is the poetry editor of the *North Dakota Quarterly*.

## PRAISE FOR DONALD JUNKINS

About Donald Junkins' 9th book of poems: *Journey to the Corrida*:

"Junkins' poems are his tribute to Spain, and then his own experiences and imagination . . . No anxiety of influence here; simply inspiration and hidden tribute, and finely written lyrics. The poems . . . are domestic, downeast, salty, familial, and precise . . . . topics range from Euripides' *Andromache* (which Junkins translated in the University of Pennsylvania Press series) to poems set in Spain, in Italy, in China, in Maine, in Michigan, in Bimini."

—Robert Lewis, *North Dakota Quarterly*

"We see again the unmistakable Junkins poise and persistence in pursuit of suppressed connections, hidden emotions and runaway home truths. Stylistic brilliance enables him to capture the slow accretion, the sudden jolt, the sheer thrill of the mind grasping what is simultaneously happening within and outside itself. Poems that begin as benign or quirky intimations in a real landscape he sees through to some haunting destinations, always mindful of his own newly-minted proverb: 'In dreams the dead talk/ straight to the heart.' Junkins' Corrida is a gutsy and elegant performance."

—Robert Bagg, *The Scrawny Sonnets and Other Poems*

About *Crossing by Ferry*:

"Junkins is a master craftsman: he carefully turns a phrase, makes a pause, gives just enough to snare readers into further shaping the situation for themselves."

—*Booklist*

"If poems are successful when their execution perfectly fulfills the aims of their writers, then this new collection by Donald Junkins leaves little room for complaint. Given the generally relaxed standard of technique in American poetry today, this book is carefully, even lovingly written."

—*New York Times Sunday Book Review*

About *Playing for Keeps:*

"Donald Junkins has been writing generous and sensual poems for over 30 years . . . . At once slangy, whimsical, charged with dense language, these poems pledge allegiance to diction both elastic and classical . . . poems of an individual life, a record, deliberate the entire time, genuine."

—*Northhampton Gazette*

About *The Agamenticus Poems:*

"These are fine, memorable poems that speak with the cadence of Maine and the murmur of old broken hearts and old healed ones. Agamenticus is a rounder, better-loved, truer terrain than Spoon River, and much closer to home."

—*The Boston Globe*

About *The Sunfish and the Partridge:*

"I don't know how Pym-Randall Press keeps snaring books that would be a credit to a New York publishing house. Donald Junkins' first collection is a strong and satisfying one. He has lived widely and deeply. Surely 'Walden, 100 Years After Thoreau' is a sequence that belongs in any good contemporary anthology."

—X.J. Kennedy

About *Andromache:*

"Andromache . . . in Junkins' translation, manages to be both lovely and dignified."

—*New York Times Sunday Book Review*

". . . a terrific work . . . the language lively, fresh and contemporary without its being faddish or slangy—it sounds like real, contemporary English being spoken with urgency. . . . This text is so alive it should last for a very long time."

—George Keithley, *The Donner Party*